BiTe SiZeD Archie®

Publisher / Co-CEO: Jon Goldwater
President / Editor-In-Chief: Mike Pellerito
Chief Creative Officer: Roberto Aguirre-Sacasa
Chief Operating Officer: William Mooar
Chief Financial Officer: Robert Wintle
Director: Jonathan Betancourt
Senior Director of Editorial: Jamie Lee Rotante
Production Manager: Stephen Oswald
Art Director: Vincent Lovallo
Lead Designer: Kari McLachlan
Co-CEO: Nancy Silberkleit

WRITTEN BY
RON CACACE

ILLUSTRATED BY
VINCENT LOVALLO

SENIOR DIRECTOR OF EDITORIAL · PROOFREADER
JAMIE LEE ROTANTE

ASSOCIATE EDITOR
STEPHEN OSWALD

PRESIDENT · EDITOR-IN-CHIEF
MIKE PELLERITO

COVER · BOOK DESIGN
VINCENT LOVALLO

PUBLISHER
JON GOLDWATER

MEET ARCHIE AND FRIENDS

ARCHIE ANDREWS
KIND-HEARTED, CLUMSY

JUGHEAD JONES
CALM, COOL, & HUNGRY

REGGIE MANTLE
TRICKSTER, NARCISSIST

BETTY COOPER
SWEETHEART, ENVIRONMENTALIST

VERONICA LODGE
RICH, FAMOUS

SABRINA SPELLMAN
WELL-MEANING, TEENAGE WITCH

CHUCK CLAYTON
ARTIST, COMIC COLLECTOR

JOSIE McCOY
MUSICIAN, PUSSYCAT

KEVIN KELLER
GOOD-NATURED, CHARISMATIC

TONI TOPAZ
COMPETITIVE, HUNGRY

SPIDER
SPIDER

CHERYL BLOSSOM
RICH, QUEEN BEE

Ron Cacace: This strip was actually inspired by a drawing that Vin did months before we got started on *Bite Sized Archie*. Once I saw his Jughead/Cuphead mash-up design, I couldn't get it out of my head and knew we needed to do more just like it!

Vincent Lovallo: Here are the sketches for the first strip (left)! I drew the layouts digitally, but printed them out on bristol board and inked them traditionally. I later gifted the original inked page to Ron for Christmas (below)!

No new notifications...

RC: Archie's hunched over expression is too funny. We've all been stuck in that endless loop of checking apps. Break the cycle, go outside, travel through time to the dinosaur era! Don't wait for a push.

BEHIND THE PANELS

VL: Panel three is one of my favorite poses of the whole series, but soon after I finished drawing it, I realized how lanky Archie was. I decided to lean more to the chibi style *Bite Sized Archie* is now recognized for.

VL: In late 2021, our coworker Dave suggested we make an exclusive *Bite Sized Archie* print in time for the holidays. Above you can see my three thumbnail sketches. Option "A" was the winner as seen in the final art below!

RC: Jingles looks so happy with himself. And that emotion on Archie in panel 3! It was easy for me to write a joke about not getting a new video game console because I got both of them on the first try. I've been fighting the scalpers in my own way by helping out my friends when they need consoles. I even surprised Vincent with a PS5, as a way to thank him for working with me on *Bite Sized Archie*!

VL: This takes me back! A lot has changed since this initial pitch strip. The style became more refined, the cast got bigger and the amount of locations significantly expanded! But the core of *Bite Sized Archie* remains the same: quick, simple, and fun!

Another aspect that remains unchanged is the art production process! I start with a rough layout (top left) to get the basic composition down. Then I proceed to refined pencils (top right) where details like body proportions and background elements become more clear. The inks come next (bottom left) to provide a sense of depth and weight. And lastly I lay down the colors and letters (next page) to help bring it to life!

RC: This was actually the first strip we made together! This was part of our pitch to show off how our new webcomic series would work and it got us approved! It's super simple and I just love it so much!

VL: Veronica, Betty, and Reggie character design concepts I drew before drawing the full strip! Their clothing and hair lean a bit retro/'60s style. In fact, for most of the earlier strips, I had kept the characters in the same outfits and hairstyles, similar to how cartoon characters have one set outfit. This changed in later strips to keep things fresh!

RC: We ended up changing the text bubble from Archie in the final panel after some guy had a meltdown online about a can of beans and we found a way to slyly reference it. It's likely an old and dated reference by the time you're reading this, but trust me, it was extremely topical at the time!

Jughead's Diner Reviews

SUBSCRIBE

38k subscribers

HOME   VIDEOS   PLAYLISTS   COMMUNITY   CHANNELS   ABOUT

Jughead's Meal Guide

ⓘ ⋮

0:00/20:21   CC ⚙ ⛶

Jughead's Meal Guide

1,941,000 views - 3 years ago

I'm not telling you how to live your life. I'm telling you how I live mine. Subscribe to my channel or don't, it really doesn't matter to me.

READ MORE

Uploads ▶ PLAY ALL

Food Review: Pop's Crispy Boi Sliders (New!)
3k views, 3 days ago

Burger Bandit Lore Explained (1/24)
5k views, 6 days ago

Let's Play: Fork Knife Burger Royale
9k views, 2 weeks ago

Anime Review: One Lunch Man
30k views, 1 month ago

RC: What would Jughead's YouTube channel look like if he was a real person? We jam-packed this one full of easter eggs and references to Jughead lore and even our Twitter account! We were originally planning to do one of these for each character but people started to think this channel was REAL so we decided to stick to just telling silly little stories instead.

VL: This is a favorite of mine for a few different reasons, but mainly because I got to draw Cosmo and Astra in panel four. Also, I'm not sure why I did this in my layout, but I gave Betty and Toni the scariest faces in panel three.

RC: We found a way to include the newest version of Cosmo the Mighty Martian, a personal favorite of ours, AND include reference to the mysterious "monoliths" that had the world's attention in late 2020. Did we ever discover what those things were, by the way?

BEHIND THE PANELS

A

B

C

RC: So this is one of those comics where I tried to turn a funny tweet into a conversation and it KINDA worked. It's supposed to be a mix of funny/weird but it ended up going more weird than funny. Anyway, when you see an airplane flying overhead, just think about it this way: there are 100+ people sitting in chairs thousands of feet above and the odds are good that one person is sitting on a toilet. I just think that's funny!!

VL: I'm so glad Ron thought to write this. The crosshatch mark on Archie's hair always looked like a hashtag to me. This whole interaction between Jughead and Archie takes it to the next level, I love it!

RC: Turning Archie's trademark hair pattern into a hashtag is not an original idea of mine but it's never been played with in an actual comic of ours before! Vin absolutely nailed the expressions on Archie's face as Jughead RIPS the hashtag off his head and breaks the "fourth wall" in the process!

VL: In the last panel of the final art, you can see a sliver of Ron to the left of Reggie, and a sliver of myself on the right! It's cut off here, but Ron's descriptor reads "Most likely to become a meme" and mine reads "Most likely to draw this strip"!

RC: Just to make things ABSOLUTELY CLEAR here: Reggie is always mucking things up and we're making fun of him for it. But you shouldn't make fun of your friends for making typos. That's not kind.

VL: Just like Archie, one of my best friends has a history of hilarious drive-through moments, including asking for all of McDonald's apple pies. He recieved seven and was extremely disappointed. Anyway, I thought of him when drawing this strip! Bite Size Me!

RC: This is based on a classic Archie Comics tweet that I wrote back in 2016! So happy to rework these little jokes into a fun format for more people to enjoy (original tweet below).

me: "and so, despite Jughead's semblance of not caring, he actually cares quite a lot."
guy at drive-thru: "are you gonna order anything?"

VL: The background here is loosely based on the kitchen in my parents' house!

RC: We've all been in this exact situation before. Too many times to count!

VL: I didn't fully sketch it out initially, but Jughead's pose in panel 1 is a reference to Edvard Munch's iconic artwork known as "The Scream."

RC: The animal in the final panel is "tiktaalik" and is believed to be our shared ancestor, the first fish to walk on land. And according to certain people, like Jughead here, the beast responsible for all our problems in the current day.

The chalkboard that Jughead is standing in front of contains references to tweets I've written, Archie's 80th anniversary, and some projects that were in development at the time!

VL: Of course Jughead has a Cosmo-inspired headset! I also chose to flip the last panel in the final version to keep Jughead's position the same from panel to panel.

RC: Putting a spin on the classic "Archie has two dates on the same night" trope by having Jughead be the one with two engagements... but they're engagements for playing video games, of course. How do you choose when two people want to play together with you on different games? It's something that haunts me daily.

VL: Sabrina's hands in panel 2 are directly referenced from another witch that appears on the cover of Archie Comics' classic horror comic, *Chilling Adventures in Sorcery!* (See bottom right)

RC: Printers are a dreadful piece of technology and you're always better off just buying a new one when your current one stops working. Vin blew everyone away with this comic, referencing the incredible color palette and panel layout of *Afterlife with Archie* artist Francesco Francavilla.

VL: Josie's design concept! I thought it'd be cute to have Josie's hands hang out like cat paws, this posing is often seen by cat-like characters in manga or anime. Both Ron and I love manga/anime and you should too!

RC: The idea of Josie being tired of all the attention that comes with being a famous musician, while also refusing to wear anything but her iconic costume while out in public, made me laugh. And if it makes me laugh, I write about it and hope that other people laugh too!

VL: I like to think that Reggie drove his motorcycle in that laid back position with his feet steering.

RC: My wife got me really into K-pop over the last couple of years and there's this great music video by RAIN and JYP called "Switch to Me" that was the inspiration for this strip. Two dudes, totally obsessed over a girl, turn that obsession into a competition with one another, and lose out to a third party at the end. That's the secret origin of this strip. That, and I wanted an excuse to see Vin draw a Reggie Mech.

VL: Betty's outfit is a nod to Misty from *Pokemon* and Archie's is a nod to Dipper from *Gravity Falls*. Why? Because I like those things, that's why.

RC: This strip is where we really started hitting our stride and I felt a lot more comfortable with writing scripts and working with Vin in giving him reference and framing. Look at that incredible background and mountain setting! Taking the Archie characters out of their town and into a new locale was so much fun. The final panel is a reference to an infamous skit from the Comedy Central show *Key & Peele*. Look it up when you're older, kids.

VL: You have to admit, the production value is pretty high for a school news team! Just look at those outfits and title cards!

RC: One of my goals for this comic was for us to find a way to not only create a weekly comic, but create content that people can use and share across the internet, outside of the context of our comic. The third panel here fits that bill perfectly, and I've seen it pop up online in the profile pictures of strangers or as a reply to an extraordinarily bad tweet. As always, Jughead Was Right.

VL: This is spider. And he's here to stay.

RC: Could this be the most important *Bite Sized Archie* ever? Not only did it feature the first appearance of Bite Sized Cheryl Blossom, it also is the first appearance of Spider! We originally didn't see Spider make it out of Cheryl's mansion... until a note from our CEO/Publisher Jon Goldwater suggested that we see him survive. We made the quick edit and as you'll see in many of the strips ahead, Spider continues to make his presence known all across Riverdale!

BEHIND THE PANELS

VL: Mr. Weatherbee is one of the only two adult characters to appear in *Bite Sized Archie* at the time of this collection's production!

RC: Archie Andrews was first introduced in 1941 and he's been a teenager pretty much ever since. We've seen him celebrate Christmas over 80 different times... How does that work? It's very simple: the sliding timeline. It explains everything!

BEHIND THE PANELS

VL: I will be forever grateful to Ron for not only reintroducing everyone's favorite cosplaying otaku Randolph, but also allowing me the opportunity to parody one of my favorite manga/anime series!

RC: There's SO much going on with this one! Panel 1 is a direct homage to a classic 1990s *Jughead* comic. Randolph, Riverdale's resident otaku, makes his *Bite Sized Archie* debut. And of course, we have the incredible *My Hero Academia* parody art by Vin! So amazing.

VL: I love the monster cereal mascots and I'm so glad Ron found a way to sorta sneak one in here. Also, I named our little amphibian friend in panel two Froginson Tadpolino.

RC: For those who might not know, Archie Comics has been publishing a line of Horror titles for almost a decade! One of those comics is called *Vampironica* and it features Veronica as, you guessed it, a vampire. When I realized we could make a few puns by including her in the series (Bite Sized Vampironica! Get it?) I knew we had to do something. And the idea of Vampironica hunting down "a Dracula" and mistakenly going after a chocolate cereal mascot was too good to pass up.

BEHIND THE PANELS

VL: I snuck myself and my fiancée Deanna buying ramen at the mall B&V visit in panel 3. It's also a true fact that we got ramen at a mall once, and it was really OK!

RC: I grew up in a small town where everything was within walking distance. This more often than not led to my group of friends hanging out at 3-4 different locations in the same night as we were constantly looking for the next "fun" thing to do. We should have realized we were having fun just being together!

VL: The poster behind Archie is a redraw of a variant cover I had the pleasure of making for the 2018 *Cosmo* revival series!

RC: This comic really riled some people up! We wanted to make a direct reference to a moment from *Riverdale* featuring Archie and Betty but add a big comedic element to it. The brick coming through the window in the final panel was not in the original script! I had some friends over for lunch and showed them the comic and asked for their feedback. I felt like the original panel didn't land with enough of a punch and thought, "What if Betty throws a brick through Archie's window?" It's the perfect ending.

VL: Sabrina's outfit colors here are the same as they were in the '70s animated series!

RC: If you've got a cat in your house, you've probably experienced this. How can something so small weigh so much? I also relished the chance to establish that Toni, Cheryl, and Sabrina are pals and all hang out together.

VL: For the final art in panel three, I decided to reference Rex Lindsey's amazing cover art to issue 2 of the original *Jughead's Time Police* series. If you haven't read it or the awesome 2019 revamp, I highly recommend!

RC: If you've never read *Jughead's Time Police* before, you need to change that immediately. There's a classic series from the '90s that introduced the descendant of Archie Andrews, January McAndrews, and featured all kinds of time traveling shenanigans. And there's a more recent series by Sina Grace and Derek Charm that features a whole host of different Jugheads fighting one another with the entire timeline at stake. It's tremendous fun and when we saw the trailer for Marvel's *Loki* series, we thought it'd be a good opportunity to point out some of the similarities between them!

VL: I underestimated how much Randolph's balloon would take up panel two. You can see from the sketch to final that I had to bump the art down to fit his long-winded speech. I do love how it came out though!

ZIP

HEY CHUCK, HAVE YOU SEEN BETTY OR VERONICA OR CHERYL OR JOSIE OR VALERIE OR SABRINA AROUND?

NOPE, I'VE BEEN WORK-

BYE!

WOOSH

AND ON PAGE 3, PANEL 2, WHEN YOU HAD TWO CHARACTERS TALKING TO ONE ANOTHER, IS THAT A JUJU REFERENCE? PAGE 7 ALSO HAS A MOMENT WHERE TWO OF THE CHARACTERS MAKE EYE CONTACT, IS IT OFFICIAL THAT THEY'RE NOW A COUPLE IN CANON? I'M CURRENTLY DEBATING THIS IN 3 DIFFERENT GROUP CHATS SO IF YOU COULD PLEASE PROVIDE AN OFFICIAL IN-UNIVERSE EXPLANATION OF THEIR RELATIONSHIP IT WOULD BE GREATLY APPRECIATED AND I CAN UPDATE THE OFFICIAL WIKI PAGE.

YES, IT'S ALL CANON, RANDOLPH!

YOU SHOULD DO A COMIC ABOUT ME! STARRING ME AND FEATURING ME! IT'LL BE HUGE!

CHUCK CLAYTON'S COOL COMICS!

JUST LIKE YOUR EGO, REGGIE!

YOUR ART IS AMAZING, WHAT'S YOUR SECRET?

CHUCK CLAYTON'S COOL COMICS!

PATIENCE!

RC: Before I started working at Archie, I worked at a comic book shop. There are all kinds of interesting conversations with customers but you can usually file them under a few themes. People who don't know how they got in the store, superfans who want to talk until your ears fall off, and people obsessed with their own stories. And, of course, the amazing folks who read and appreciate the comics and the art form.

VL: Some folks have clunkers, some have hot rods, and apparently some have tanks! Thanks to all the superstar parents or guardians out there that would do this for their kid (even though it's just a *little* excessive)!

RC: We wanted to feature Kevin in one of our strips for Pride Month and the idea of his father, an overly enthusiastic and supportive Army guy picking his son up from school in a tank, was too good to pass up.

VL: In the final art, if you look super close at the phone and its after images in panel four, you can see the notifications number increase. Each number is actually a date or year reference that is either significant to me or Archie Comics in general. For example, the middle phone shows the date I started interning at Archie (1/5/2011)!

RC: Going viral on social media is a gift and a curse. It's incredible to see a wave of positive responses flow in that show you that something you posted is being rewarded with attention... until that attention escapes the people who have the context of who you are and what you've written. Once people start misinterpreting your viral post or using it to get their own message viral, the best thing to do is throw your phone into the ocean and walk away.

VL: Ron educated me on what a phone farm was prior to drawing panel four. Don't plant your SIM card in soil and water it, it's not a good idea.

RC: My wife Amelia is a huge fan of the Korean K-pop group TWICE and we even got to see them in concert when they did their first US tour. I wanted to incorporate our love of K-pop into the strip... and Reggie Mantle being a secret K-pop fan who uses Dilton's computer skills to rig a contest was just too funny to me.

VL: You may have noticed that Archie and Jughead are floating in mid-air! That's because I added in the Pop's diner background at the coloring phase. I keep it as it's own separte layer since we return to the setting quite often!

RC: "Don't bite off more than you can chew," is a saying for a reason. In this case, the burger was simply too big for Jughead to handle. I've had this exact thing happen to me more often than I'd like to admit and it's quite painful.

VL: You all know the meme. I drew this for fun the day the strip went live.

RC: The Archie Comics characters are over 80 years old.
Star Wars: Attack of the Clones is 20 years old.
I don't know how old you are but I bet you're feeling a little bit older after reading those two facts.

VL: Not in the original script, but as I was reading the layout for Archie's team I envisioned Jughead balancing a dodgeball on his nose like a dolphin. I think it worked out swimmingly!

RC: There's a super fun video game called *Knockout City* and I was definitely obsessed with it for a while, which led directly to the inspiration for this strip. Vin picked out the players for Harvey's squad, including Ren and Shinji, and added the little chibi Sabrina inset in the final panel. One of my favorite strips we've worked on together!

BEHIND THE PANELS

VL: Not in the original sketches, but I knew I'd be filling Chuck's room with a lot of anime and video game posters. Some are holdovers from previous strips and some are new! Can you identify what popular franchises were referenced?

RC: Actual photos of my comic collection dressed up like a bed.

RC: This is based on a somewhat true story. My extremely large comic book collection had been in my dad's house for years and when he was getting ready to sell the home, he needed to either get the boxes out or cover them up somehow. We made the boxes look like a bed and the comic book bed even made it into the real estate listing.

VL: Random detail: when I read that the setting was the school gym I immediatley thought back to my own high school gym that had these neat, ergonomic, pull-out bleachers affixed to the wall, so I drew them in here for the kids to lean on!

RC: Playing with expectations and character pairings is always fun. You know what else is fun? Breaking the fourth wall. This one got a bunch of funny reactions online and Vin did such a great job with the amazing outfits, which were inspired by Audrey Mok's incredible and iconic cover to *Archie* #30.

VL: Not as common as Spider, but I will often sneak Cosmo into the strips if I can and it makes sense. Ron wrote for panel four, "Cheryl is sitting at a desk, looking at a computer monitor, with dozens of RED items behind her. Red shoes, red dresses, red apples, red toy cars, etc." so naturally I leaped at the opportunity!

RC: The debut of Bite Sized Midge! Cheryl Blossom being iconic! A subtle meme! The return of Spider! This one was so much fun to write. Vin really did an amazing job with Cheryl's smug face in panel 4!

BEHIND THE PANELS

VL: I'm one of the few people Archie that isn't a die-hard wrestling fan. That doesn't mean I don't like it, I just never really followed it closely. I do love the idea that wrestlers take on colorful personas like comic book heroes, so Ron writing Archie as Pureheart being a wrestler is just perfection.

RC: I've always been a huge fan of wrestling! Shortly after I started working at Archie Comics in 2014, a WWE Superstar named Sami Zayn went on the *Talk is Jericho* podcast and revealed that he was an avid reader of Archie Comics. We ended up sending him a box of comics and I even got to meet him at San Diego Comic-Con in 2015! This comic is dedicated to Sami and the character he played before he made it to WWE. Also, there's a *Daredevil* easter egg with Archie's shirt in panel 4.

VL: As I was drawing this, I realized this was the first time Hot Dog would appear in *Bite Sized Archie*! I thought it would be cute if Jughead and Hot Dog shared the same expressions, echoing the timeless "dogs mirror their owners" thing.

RC: Longtime viewers of *The Simpsons* will likely recognize the car in this strip. In Season 6, Episode 5, Homer Simpson is kicked out of Archie's jalopy and told to "Stay out of Riverdale" by Archie and pals. It's never explained beyond that moment but it's something that's always stuck with me and I wanted to find a way to pay homage to that scene. Flipping the circumstances and having Archie get dropped off at his house after spending the day in Springfield felt like the right move.

VL: When Ron told me we were going to be referencing *The Shining* I was immediately on board. For the last panel, I wanted to take it one step beyond and really push the retro designs and hairstyles for the cast. It was a lot of fun to change things up! Remember, no burgers and no shakes makes Jughead a dull boy...

RC: A combination of multiple pop culture references and a celebration of the 80-year legacy of Archie Comics all in one. The photo at the end is a direct reference to the end of *The Shining* (kids, ask your parents!) and the idea of Jughead eating burgers forever and ever is a reference to another *Key & Peele* skit ("Continental Breakfast") which itself was referencing *The Shining*. There are layers upon layers here!

VL: No shoobies allowed at this skate park!

RC: Sometimes I'll picture the last panel of a comic, what's essentially the punchline of the joke, and have to figure out a way to get there. My wife is a teacher and she was telling me about this one kid who, whenever he comes back from the playground, always has a bunch of rocks in his pants. Why are the rocks there? Well, he keeps putting them there! So the idea of Archie and Reggie having a contest to see who can store the most rocks in their pants was something I knew we had to do... but I wanted it to come out of left field! We've been partnered with the folks at Everyone Skateboards to do custom skateboard decks with iconic Archie artwork and I'm always seeing young people skating around my neighborhood. The idea that the boys are all off doing something silly while the girls are shredding it up at the skatepark just felt right.

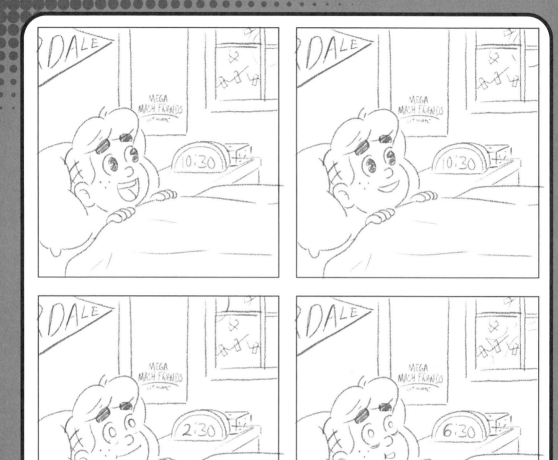

VL: Ron does brilliant work of making these strips relatable, even when you wish you didn't relate to them! Also, I made sure to call back to strip #25 with the broken window and the brick next to Archie's alarm clock. Archie is clearly still holding a torch for Betty!

RC: I love sleeping but I hate the process of falling asleep. I have to go and pretend to be asleep in order to fall asleep? When my head hits the pillow, I tend to immediately think about the things I have to do when I wake up, and it keeps me up later than I'd like to be. I figured, let's see Archie struggle with this on the night of a big test. Vin did a great job on the 'Mega Mash Pals Ultimate' poster in the background, using some really deep-cut characters from the Archie library in his art!

VL: Jughead was triumphant. A huge success.
It's hard to overstate his satisfaction.

RC: You might start to notice a trend where me and Vin incorporate lots of video game humor/references into these comics. We're both big gamers and Archie Comics have always incorporated pop culture and trends into storylines. *Splitgate*, a new game that's a combination of *Halo* and *Portal*, really took things by storm in 2021 and this strip is dedicated to the game. What would you do if you had a portal glove?

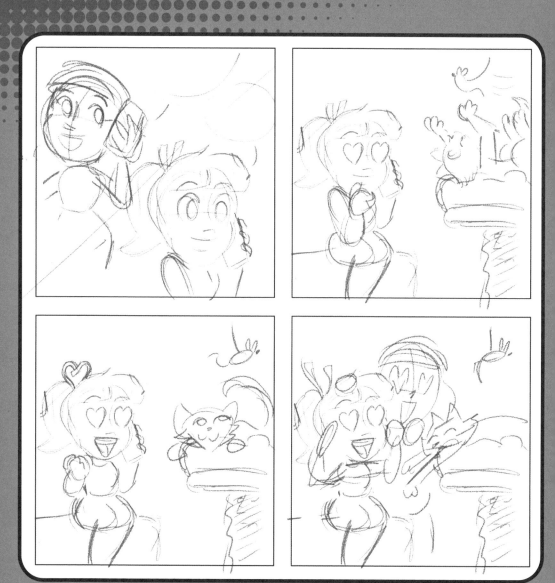

VL: Caramel's pose in panel 4 is modeled after my parents' cat, who often will stretch her arms out in her sleep. I wonder if she dreams of being a flying super-cat?

RC: In the script for this comic I asked Vin to draw "Caramel the cat doing something super cute." And he delivered! Plus, another appearance from Spider! How many strips has Spider popped up in so far? You'll have to look closely to figure that out!

VL: I'm just so pleased with how Archie's bear impersonation came out. His face ended up being perfect for an emoji.

RC: Plenty of references in this strip, from Archie's off-screen battle with a bear from The CW's *Riverdale* series to Betty's outfit looking very close to a certain bounty hunter from a popular video game series... We really had a bunch of fun with this one!

VL: Don't worry, we didn't use CGI on any of these cat people.

RC: I knew we needed to get Josie and the Pussycats involved more in this series, especially since Vin had Josie on the cover, so I was really happy with how this one turned out. The layout of the first three panels is a reference to Veronica Fish's amazing variant cover for the *Josie and the Pussycats* reboot in 2016. Archie and Reggie being dressed as the Pussycats is a reference to an infamous photo of KJ Apa and Charles Melton (*Riverdale*'s Archie & Reggie) that you can see for yourself online.

VL: Salem was originally going to be sitting next to Sabrina, but when I was placing the word balloons, I realized he had to be removed. Sorry, Mr. Saberhagen.

RC: How do you reference memes without coming across as desperate or out-of-touch? That's been a huge priority for us to figure out because these comics are designed to be shared on social media. People see right through disingenuous attempts at fitting in but thankfully whenever we do these comics, people seem to understand and appreciate them!

VL: Reggie is so full of himself that he even had a lamp custom made in his image to brighten up his room!

RC: Not a day goes by that I don't get multiple spam phone calls! It's really gotten to the point where you never want to pick up the phone at all! Oh, and check out Spider in panel 2 hanging from Reggie's lampshade!

BEHIND THE PANELS

VL: Since Chuck is Riverdale's resident comic book aficionado, I felt that it would make sense to toss in a few of the other classic Archie Comics characters from the past! The kids in panel 3 are none other than Pipsqueak (first appearing in *The Adventures of... Pipsqueak* #34) and Li'l Jinx (first appearing in *Pep Comics* #62)!

RC: This comic is based on a partially true story. During the Fall of 2021, my town was holding these pop-up markets on the main street where people could sell arts, crafts, and other goods. I have an absolutely massive comic book collection (you saw the boxes earlier, right?) and was looking for a way to unload some of them. Well, one night, while picking my wife up from work, I accidentally opened my trunk and forgot to close it. Normally, this wouldn't be a problem, but on this night, I had boxes full of comics in there! When we got home a few minutes later, we saw that I had left a trail of comic books for several blocks! The good news: they weren't heavily damaged and we were able to recover all of them safely. And now I had a great idea for a comic!

VL: For this strip I decided to give the final art a slight blur effect to further emphasize the '80s anime vibe we were going for. I also kept the rain on a separate layer so that I could animate for fun later.

RC: My wife loves *My Neighbor Totoro* and somehow the image of Sabrina and Salem waiting at the iconic bus stop came to me... I knew we had something there. Vin did an incredible job with the image and we were able to have this comic debut right around the time of the *Riverdale* Season 6 premiere, as fans were eagerly anticipating Sabrina's debut on the show. One of my favorite comics that we've ever done!

VL: I decided to slightly reference the "Y U NO" guy for Archie's pose in panel 2.

RC: You always need to be careful with the information you share on the internet, especially if you're sharing a personal opinion. People can be ruthless, even in the normally friendly town of Riverdale!

VL: A year's worth of strips all came down to this! In the first draft, Ron originally scripted this strip as one large panel, which became panel 4 in the final version. After discussing we agreed it would be appropriate to bring Archie and Jughead back to where it all started: The big tree where this little webcomic series continued to grow!

RC: And here it is... the final comic of the collection, which also marks a full year of published stories. The artwork here is repurposed from the first comic that Vin and I ever worked on together, which was the pitch to get *Bite Sized Archie* approved and into production.
The final panel features the two of us... asking you to buy the book that you're reading right now! Thanks so much for reading this collection and please be sure to follow the @ArchieComics social media accounts to read new editions of *Bite Sized Archie* every Friday!

AFTERWORD

"Let's make a webcomic!"

It's a simple enough idea...

And yet it somehow hasn't been done before here at Archie Comics.

We've had one-off comics posted on our social media here and there and we've even created digital exclusive content. But a weekly webcomic series designed and published with our online audience in mind, featuring our entire assortment of characters? It's never been done before.

...Until now!

You've just read the first collection of *Bite Sized Archie*, a new webcomic series created by comic fans, for comic fans.

The 52 comics collected in this volume represent the first year of collaboration between myself and artist Vincent Lovallo. Vin's artwork is simultaneously bold, bright, and expressive, while also remaining recognizably "Archie." It's not an easy balance to achieve but Vin is absolutely crushing it on these comics and I'm so thankful to be working with him.

We wanted to make a comic series that was cute, simple, quirky, and relatable, while being genuinely "us." And I think we've hit that goal.

We hope you enjoyed reading this collection and if you want to read more, be sure to follow @ArchieComics on Twitter, Instagram, and Facebook and use the hashtag #BiteSizedArchie when discussing these comics on social media!

Ron Cacace
Writer, *Bite Sized Archie*

THANKS TO THE FANS

Since *Bite Sized Archie* launched in late 2020, we've seen an outpour of love and support from veteran and new Archie Comics fans alike! We are overjoyed by the kind words, stories, and fan art the fans have shared with us, and are so happy to see that *Bite Sized Archie* has become a source of inspiration to you all. From the bottom of our hearts, thank you so much for your support and for sharing your talents with us!

Vincent Lovallo
Artist, *Bite Sized Archie*

Veeti A.

R.Case

Corey L.

Noviembre B.

Daphne S-V.'s boys
Will, Sam, and Ben

Leslie S.

ABOUT THE WRITER

RON CACACE

Ron Cacace first logged on the internet at the age of 8 years old and he has never recovered. His love for comic books started early and led him to making fan comics, working at a comic book shop, interning at Marvel Entertainment, and eventually running the social media and publicity efforts at Archie Comics. Ron is best known for shaping the online image of the Archie Comics brand and finding new ways to engage with fans and readers. He is also known for that time he made a bunch of professional newscasters say the phrase "i'm baby" on national television. Ron lives in New Jersey with his wife and cat.

ABOUT THE ARTIST

VINCENT LOVALLO

Vincent Lovallo is a New York-based illustrator, editor, and art director with a passion for all-ages stories. At Archie Comic Publications, Inc., Vincent has overseen production on dozens of action-adventure titles such as *Jughead's Time Police* and *Cosmo the Mighty Martian*. He is the artist behind *Bite Sized Archie*, Archie Comics' very first webcomic series, *Heebie Jeebies* on WEBTOON, and was responsible for updating the design of Playland's mascot, Coaster the Dragon for the Westchester-based amusement park. In his spare time, Vincent enjoys drawing, reading comics, playing video games, and watching movies, especially animated features.